LIVING IN THE PAST

[handwritten inscription:] To Rose — with great affection and respect *[signature]*

LIVING IN THE PAST

Poems

Philip Schultz

HARCOURT, INC.

Orlando ★ Austin ★ New York ★ San Diego ★ Toronto ★ London

www.HarcourtBooks.com

Library of Congress Cataloging-in-Publication Data
Schultz, Philip.
Living in the past: poems / Philip Schultz.—1st ed.
p.   cm.
ISBN 0-15-100872-8
1. Boys—Poetry. 2. Bar mitzvah—Poetry. 3. Jewish families—Poetry.
4. Ethnic relations—Poetry. 5. Rochester (N.Y.)—Poetry.
6. Jews—New York (State)—Rochester—Poetry.   I. Title.
PS3569.C5533L58   2004
811'.54—dc22   2003021438

Text set in Dante
Designed by Scott Piehl

Printed in the United States of America
First edition

A C E G I K J H F D B

For Elli

Remember: Thou art what thou art. On a hot day,
drink a lot of water—chug it down and change.

Yehuda Amichai

CONTENTS

PART IV

LIVING IN THE PAST

PART I

You hear me speak. But do you hear me feel?

Gertrud Kolmar

I

The Ukrainians hate the Romanians while the Poles hate the Germans
but especially the Italians who hate the blacks who haven't even
moved into the neighborhood yet, while Grandma hates mostly
the Russians who are Cossacks who piss on everyone's tomatoes
and wag their tongues at everyone's wives. She even hates her Lithuanian
blue eyes and turnip Russian nose and fat Polish tongue; sometimes
she forgets what she hates most and ends up hating everything about herself.
This is Rochester, N.Y., in the fifties, when all the Displaced Persons
move in and suddenly even the elms look defeated. Grandma believes
they came here so we all could suffer, that soon we'll all dress
like undertakers and march around whispering to the dead.

2

No one in this family ever suspects they're unhappy;
in fact, the less happy we are, the less we suspect it.
Uncle walks around with a straightedge razor tied round
his neck on a red string, screaming and pounding on things.
When he's angry, and he's always angry, he drops to a crouch
and screams until the veins in his neck bulge like steam pipes.
Mother locks herself, Grandma, and me in the toilet until he's flat.
We spend a lot of time in the toilet never suspecting anything.
Didn't everyone on Cuba Place have an uncle who hides
in a tiny room off the kitchen yelling at a police radio and writing
letters to dead presidents while reading girlie books all night?
Didn't everyone live in a house where everyone feels cheated,
ignored, and unredeemed?

3

Grandma climbs a chair to yell at God for killing
her only husband whose only crime was forgetting
where he put things. Finally, God misplaced him. Everyone
in this house is a razor, a police radio, a bulging vein.
It's too late for any of us, Grandma says to the ceiling.
She believes we are chosen to be disgraced and perplexed.
She squints at anyone who treats her like a customer, including
the toilet mirror, and twists her mouth into a deadly scheme.
Late at night I run at the mirror until I disappear. The day is over
before it begins, Grandma says, jerking the shade down over
its once rosy eye. She keeps her husband's teeth in a matchbox,
in perfumed paraffin; his silk skullcap (with its orthodox stains)
in the icebox, behind Uncle's Jell-O aquarium of floating lowlifes.
I know what Mrs. Einhorn said Mrs. Edels told Mr. Kook about us:
God save us from having one shirt, one eye, one child. I know
in order to survive. Grandma throws her shawl of exuberant birds
over her bony shoulders and ladles up yet another chicken thigh
out of the steaming broth of the infinite night sky.

4

Grandma peeps from behind her shades at everyone peeping at her.
The Italians are having people over in broad daylight, while the Slovaks
are grilling goats alive (this means a ten-year stink!), and the Ukrainians
are mingling on their porches, plotting our downfall. "Keep out of my yard,"
she cries in her sleep. Everyone sneaks around, has a hiding place.
Uncle's police radio calls all cars to a virgin abducted on Main Street,
while Mother binges on Almond Joys and Father sleepwalks through
the wilderness of the living room, Odysseus disguised as a Zionist,
or a pickled beet—"With my hands in my pockets and my pockets in my pants
watch the little girlies do the hootchie koochie dance!" he sings every morning.
Nights, I sneak into the toilet, where Uncle jumps out of the tub, yelling "Boo!"
I hide behind my eyes where even I can't find me.

5

Old man Haas next door dresses in soiled sheets and sacrifices cats
in his backyard, whispering Grandma's maiden name. He wants us
gassed even if Hitler isn't going to invade Cuba Place. Nazis
are fortune-tellers and know everyone's secrets, Grandma thinks.
Bubbe, I say, either he's a Nazi or a Grand Wizard, he can't be both,
nobody's that evil! Good for him, she says, now he'll burn in hell
only five thousand years. He stands in the alley between our houses
snapping hedge shears, daring me to get past him, just once. One day
he steps on something Grandma drops in a dream and comes home
from the hospital with two empty pant legs and now Grandma
won't even look at the ceiling because what God gives with
the right hand he takes with the left.

6

Mother locks me and Grandma in the toilet until Uncle stops
pulverizing the door because one of the cashiers at the Paramount
looked at him funny and he pulled the curtain shut on Humphrey Bogart
and the bus driver didn't say hello again. I'm sick of hiding with Grandma
who spits on Mrs. Tillem's older sister Etta for giving her the evil eye
in the Quality Bakery in front of Mrs. Epstein who's there every time
something bad happens. Let something good happen and even Hitler
can't find her. I don't know about Mrs. Epstein, but I'm sick of waiting
like Grandma for the cherubim to deliver us out of Egypt just so
we can tell everyone to go to Hell.

7

Grandma ties red strings to doorknobs, chairs, lamps, both her thumbs
because Mrs. Tillem complimented her hat, and now she has a nosebleed,
and old man Haas screams "Lousy Hebes" in his sleep as his swastika
lights blink in every window, and all four daughters (named Babe) goose-step
round the neighborhood, while Mr. Hildebrand's two three-legged reindeer
race up his roof toward statuesque bliss. Cossacks hung Grandma's cousin
Leopold's balls over the door like mistletoe. That's why she hates a season
that smells so good and never crosses her legs or eyes or shows anyone
her profile, why she opens her mouth only to scream, because dibbuks enter
us through the mouth, and she hates being a landlord even to the dead.

8

Uncle likes to look at naked women do the limbo,
their flesh curled like diplomas, their shrewd crocus bellies
and recondite shoulders and tugboat hips towing salutations,
their breasts a private alphabet, improvising beautiful soliloquies,
their hair piled high into platinum high-rises. Me? I also sneak
into the attic to wonder why they squint sphinxlike, own such
recrudescent seamless flesh that makes even God blush. Uncle
smuggles shopping bags back and forth in the dark like refugees.
I think he thinks they know his name, are his guardian angels.
Sometimes at night he screams: "Oh lordy lord hallelujah please!"

9

Grandma says Rabbi Epstein isn't a real rebbe but an assistant mohel
because he cut Mrs. Kreiger's only boy's future half an inch too close.
His only son Mendel is let out only on weekends so he can walk up
and down the street with his hands locked behind his head, humming
Yiddish wedding songs. Ah, Mendel's more crazy than even the DP's
who rock themselves dizzy on every porch on Cuba Place. Like an army
of golems, Grandma says, they've come to steal the breath from our lungs.
Everybody blames everybody else but Grandma knows whose fault they are—
when God turned a deaf ear Mrs. Kreiger hired the devil and now Mendel
leads the lunatic parade up and down Cuba Place . . . children follow him
making fun but I leave him alone because, Grandma says, a boil under
someone else's arm isn't hard to bear. Still, I stay away
from Rabbi Epstein's house after dark.

IO

Almost every night Mr. Schwartzman wakes up Spinoza calm
in a pit named Auschwitz, opens his Lazarus eyes wide and looks
around at the dead eyeballs, broken fingers and mouths stuffed
with screams, his teeth tick, his kneecaps scrape, his nose big
as a blood sausage. For piano lessons I write his letters nobody answers,
about Mrs. Tillem's boardinghouse, where everybody stinks of herring
and moans in their sleep; about his job at the A & P providing for
everyone else's appetite. Not about what happened to his music or why
God spared him. Saturday mornings for two years he speaks Yiddish
as I write my twelve-year-old English until the day I find him hanging
in his closet with a note pinned to his tie: "One does not perish among Jews."

II

Everyone dickers with God. Everyone gets something.
Grandma gets one dead husband who does nothing
but read Torah and complain, the kitchen ceiling where
all her curses live rent free, a lifetime of oy veis. . . . Uncle gets
his wieners, eight varieties of sauerkraut, five newspapers spread
over the kitchen table like a vast strategy, the Paramount screen
where he pulls curtains shut on Marlene D who shaves her legs
four times a day. Father gets free room and board, a coal-burner
to intimidate, all the blame. Mother gets the lower left half of
the icebox, where she hides bacon, Popsicles, all her glee.
I get the best hiding places, Uncle's girlie books, the stained glass
attic window where the wind sings of inner and outer things,
as Martin Buber said, what are they but things—"O secrecy
without a secret! O accumulation of information!" I get faith
and intuition and 5,763 years of longing and despair, a passion
for hearsay, boogying and epistemology . . .

12

Before Uncle burned Grandma's house down
he burned down the Dubinsky brothers' junkyard barn
because he used to climb our roof to watch their sister
dance naked in her bedroom. Grandma says only a Russian slut
doesn't know to pull a shade over her big teats when she dances
for the devil. Everybody on Cuba Place watches her but they
only knock Uncle's teeth out. She blames God for putting
a junkyard behind our house. Uncle blames only the barn.
When he burns her house down in the middle of the night
she says only one word, she says, "See!"

PART II

So I will step beneath my fate . . . even though I do not know what it will be: I have accepted it in advance, I have given myself up to it, and know it will not crush me, will not find me too small. How many . . . who break down . . . have asked themselves whether they do not deserve some punishment, whether they must not atone for something? I was no worse than other women . . . but I knew I did not live the way I should have, and I was always ready to do penance.

Gertrud Kolmar
(Letter of December 15, 1942, Auschwitz)

13

Mr. Schwartzman survived the Nazis but not Cuba Place, where
he takes long Saturday walks with his five dead children
who ride a carousel round the inside of his cracked eyeballs,
each a continent, a resume filed at Auschwitz, where Gertrud Kolmar,
his older sister's best friend, also was murdered, her poems
scratched in blood, flying over the Urals, singing, "Out of darkness
I come, a woman, I carry a child, and have forgotten whose it is."
He reads her at the back of his candlelit eyes, his kaddish voice
wears a tallis and skullcap, praising her soul's dark soliloquy: "I am
a continent that will sink without a sound into the sea."

14

The Cinemascope is too big for the screen so Alan Ladd
rides off into the curtains and the gangsters in the B picture
look like the men in the pool hall where Father owns
peanut machines. The lights come on and we shake Father
and follow everyone out to walk home under the elms and
sycamores, through the crickets, fireflies and honeysuckle,
Mother's hand in mine and Father a step ahead, bent under
the streetlights whose shadows curl his fedora into a snake
and squeeze his face into a fist. Friday nights in spring nobody
talks about lugging syrup cases up factory stairs or stopping
to breathe in icy alleyways or counting greasy coins until
your thumbs blister or all the bills we can't pay.... In spring
we walk under the Rochester stars, chilled and stuck-up,
Father says, his lips silently answering old insults, Mother's
blue eyes black with a sadness she can't say, all the way
to our house on Cuba Place, where the porch light sways
in the breeze off Lake Ontario and the fence needs painting
and the kitchen sags under our weight, where Mother and I
were born and I am the best thing that ever happened to her,
she whispers, putting me to bed, back when the world was new
and Alan Ladd was already too big for the neighborhood.

15

On Saturdays I follow Father through factories, pool halls,
tool & die shops, lathes echoing off cinder block as we lug
dollies piled high with syrup, ice cream in hissing dry ice,
under blue fluorescent clouds in meat freezers, slipping in
greasy sawdust, his thumbless left hand zipping razor-edged
metal coffins, *zziiiinngggoooopppp!*, tossing in candy, cigarettes,
Mother's tuna salad, unclogging hot and cold colored snakes
inside soda and coffee machines, cursing and praying to screws
nuts and wires he means nothing to, kibbitzing over his always
moving shoulder to men in overalls and suits at DuPonts, Gerbers,
Bonds, Bausch and Lomb's (everyone a war hero!), handing out
free coffee, cashews, Mounds bars, women giggling as his big smile
swaggers down hallways . . . until we get home in the dark, stinking
of chocolate, coffee grounds, powdered sugar, soured mayonnaise,
his hands red and swollen from slapping a million backs.

16

On Wednesday mornings Grandma packs shopping bags
with potato salad, sour pickles, bundles of girlie books,
as Uncle yells, "All salami, no bologna for Izzy, Ma!"
tugging at his shoelaces under a signed photo of Mae West—
everything in his room hangs from the ceiling, police radio,
butcher knife, fountain pens, a rhyming dictionary. "It's time
SOMEBODY went to see him! Everybody acts like he's dead
but *who's* eating all this goddamn salami!" Only Grandma says
anything: "God suck the eyes out of my head and put boils
on my tongue! He who lives with a devil becomes one!"
We all know who SOMEBODY is—he wants *me* to visit
my crazy uncle Izzy at the State Hospital! Izzy, who bit
a Ukrainian woman in Levi's grocery for bending over
to taste a pickle, whom Uncle pushed off the roof for watching
the Dubinsky girl dance naked in her bedroom, which everyone
knew was his privilege, whom Grandma says kaddish for!
"Don't take it personally," Mr. Schwartzman says, rocking
on his porch with all the other DP's, "everyone needs a witness."
Nothing is personal in the middle of the twentieth century, he says,
each of us a spoonful of worm stew. In another 248 days
I'll be bar mitzvahed and leave this valley of endless weeping.

17

Grandma watched her mother watch their barn full of animals
burn down on their farm in the hills north of Vilna just like
her mother watched her mother watch crazed horsemen hang
her grandpa upside down from the oak she, my grandma's grandma,
climbed and read in on hot summer afternoons, his blood dripping
from his eyes, nose and ears as he hung like a sack of dead cats, he
the only grandpa she had left, like her mother, who said, "God
look with your own eyes and see what you've chosen us for!"

18

Being chosen doesn't mean what Grandma thinks,
Mr. Schwartzman says. It's not a boast but an obligation,
as Abraham said, a chosenness to sanctify the name of God.
"Of all the families on earth . . . will I visit upon you all your
iniquities." We are a choosing people, the dawn and the dusk,
the challenge and the test. Yes, but after everything that happened
to him, did *he* believe in God? I ask. He shuts his eyes and says:
"Spinoza believed he who revenges lives in misery and enemies
of faith are its greatest defenders, that passion without reason
is blind as reason with passion is death, that nothing we do
affects our fate and nothing is our fate. Martin Buber said,
'God's existence cannot be proved. Yet he who dares to speak
of it, bears witness. . . .' The year Columbus discovered America,
Ferdinand discovered the Jews. Thus: the Inquisition without
which there'd be no Spinoza, or a boychick on Cuba Place.
You ask what I believe? I believe in Darwin and Beethoven.
In Getrud Kolmar's longing for ecstasy and heritage, and
most of all, I believe in believing, and in Talmud there is faith
and knowledge, so according to this Gospel, I believe in God."

19

Memories talk about us behind our back, Grandma believes.
What do they care about her? She didn't give birth to them.
She never asked them to marry her. All they care about is regret
and disappointment. Let them worry about her for a change.
Let them remember the names of the songs she sang as a girl,
her childhood friends. Let them remember what her husband
called her when they danced cheek to rosy cheek. Let them
remember his hands on her hair in unwashed moonlight, the color
of his eyes that first time. Let them remember the prayers he sang
each morning and night. Let them remember themselves.

20

Every night at Kodak as he sweeps the floors,
Father dreams of the vending machines he'll buy.
He comes home after dawn and sits at the kitchen table
staring out the window, his lips silently moving.
He wants the biggest vending business in upstate
New York, that's why he buys new machines
without paying for the old ones, Mother says,
so he can be a big shot. All the things she never says
give her headaches so I rub her neck as she holds ice
to her eyes. After someone on the phone yells, she
eats ice cream and Mars bars. "What must you think
of me, crying all day? Please don't be like me, don't
agree with everyone . . ." Father falls asleep pulling
his pants off but soon there's coffee in J.C. Penney's
and five kinds of soda in Abe's Pool Hall . . . while
Uncle pays all the bills, walks around in torn boxers
making us watch TV and eat in the dark. When he
tells me to draw a "pic'chur of a horse drawin' a wagon,"
I draw a horse with a pencil in its hoof and hide as he
rips it up, raves all night. In this house, where everyone's
a genius, talks only to themselves, and spits three times
over their left shoulder, everything is a riddle.

21

Mr. Schwartzman writes fifteen letters to a dead older brother,
Reuben, who, like Spinoza, grinds eyeglasses for a living.
"God only knows why he lives in Berlin. It's a beautiful city,
long clean avenues . . . but they murdered him!" Five letters to
a dead daughter, Rebecca, who lives in Paris which is beautiful
at night, like glass, like Mozart. . . . He unbuttons his vest and sighs—
"Four children and her singing career flourishes! Sons are wonderful
but a daughter looks after you. . . . Gertrud died childless: 'Oh the stillness . . .
in my womb: the axe . . . my child.'" He keeps his letters in a shoebox
in the closet next to the bed that lives in the wall like a ghost.

22

I like to look at the photos of Mother and her girlfriends
by the Genesee River, languishing in front of lilacs in
Highland Park, posing all over Rochester like flappers
in checkered knickers and headbands and big bows.
This was her opportunity, her teachers said, but girls
didn't finish school so she worked as a filing clerk for
twenty years, until she met Father. Her eyes are shiny
as she smiles at a photo of her and her friends waving
small American flags in front of a flourishing waterfall. . . .

23

Every Saturday Mr. Schwartzman lets me sneak him
into the Paramount by knocking three times until Uncle
opens the back door. According to the movies everyone
in America is a gangster or a hero, he says. He likes
Gary Cooper because he saves everyone. God is the hero
of the Bible, but he saved almost no one. In Europe it's more
like the Bible, where everyone is asked to sacrifice something.
For what? Yetzer Ha-ra, the evil desire inherent in everyone,
lived in Abraham and also in Mr. Schwartzman, who sacrificed
a wife, all three sons and two daughters. A hero is what everyone
wanted but Gary Cooper must have been busy saving someone else.

24

We walk through the lilac stink to the front doors and
down a long hallway to the elevators which Uncle bangs
open, then down a corridor to a screened locked door
where a black man says, "Lo, Moe, you're late this week."
Uncle gives him a bundle of girlie books and leads us across
a cafeteria to a table where a small pink man licks his lips.
"Izzy, this is your nephew," Uncle says. Izzy smiles, kicking
his feet. Bald and rosy, with Mother's blue eyes and Grandma's
turnip nose, he stuffs his cheeks with everything Moe unpacks:
celery bologna pickles sardines coleslaw . . . until the black man
sticks a spoon down his throat making him gurgle and pump
out a hissing spray into a pail, a spool swinging on his chin. . . .
"Atta boy," Uncle says, uncapping a pen, "now write your name!"
Izzy writes in block letters, his face red and swollen and then
the black man takes his bundle and Izzy's hand and they go
back across the cafeteria down the long echoing linoleum.

25

When Uncle burned the house down God was doing
Grandma a favor, Rabbi Epstein said, may the worms save
his tongue for last. She shouldn't worry, because it wasn't Russia
and she didn't own cows and her husband wasn't dead for another
three years. The only thing we can look forward to, she believes,
is what we fear most because fate knows our name and every time
someone says it twice on the same day God writes it down and
if anything good happens to us the book opens to our name . . .

26

Paul Anka sings "Oh I'm just a lonely boy" as we go 90 mph
on the thruway to Brooklyn. We're on our way to my cousin's funeral,
he with the same first name, birthday, birthmark on his right ass cheek,
the same horsey laugh, as me. But I'm no albino with white eyelashes.
Five years younger, I'm convinced I'll die at eighteen, too, never know that
big walloping boomerang you do with girls, all your roosters crowing.
His only girl a vampire named Leukemia. Yet who can forget his ghost
face singing "I love you Joe DiMaggio!" under a lamplight deep
in the black humid nights of Nostrand Avenue.

27

Spuming a perish melody, Mr. Schwartzman rocks on his porch,
remembering how they lined up in cornstalk rows, his wife Dore
and sons Michael and Jacob and Nahum and daughters Rebecca
and Leah, naked on the lip of the ravine . . . one falling atop another
like stones into a black pool. . . . He recalls this because it's Shabbos
and the DP's are marching to shul like dead weights on one of God's
scales, measuring heaven, hell and everything trapped between.
He combs his bald spot left to right, picks at his liver spots, his mind
an original garden without finials whose curious leaves mirror the
genius of the universe . . . he stood there watching a monarch butterfly
in the bright spring air, its wings inviting a miracle of divine intervention. . . .

28

In winter the dark outside is less dark than the dark inside.
Moonlight crisscrosses my wall where Uncle's face floats
in a cracked riverbed and the floor creaks as the house drips,
wind scrapes its icy nails on the shingles and attic bats beat
hollow wings and the rats dance (before Father smacks them
flat and pops them in the burner) and old man Haas coughs up
his Nazi phlegm in his bedroom across the alleyway . . . and if
I listen hard enough the backyard grass trembles one Hebrew
letter at a time as the three-legged sofa says good night to
the kitchen table and Uncle's naked attic women get cozy
in their paper beds, and then, if I'm lucky, I'll sleep deep
inside the ceiling's spiderweb of shadows and stop hearing
Uncle's police radio calling all our angels back to heaven,
even on the inside of my eyelids where Izzy writes his name
in big block letters over and over and over again. . . .

29

Father waves his hands around muddy holes in the ground
staked with red flags, yelling, "Over here will be our bedroom
ceiling that'll open to the stars, and over there a ballroom with
three fireplaces and Eye-talian marble, down there a bowling alley!"
No more dirt cellars for us, we're leaving Cuba Place! Every spring
we look at empty lots, say good-bye to old man Haas and Cuba Place!
My hand disappears inside Father's big paw as we celebrate with
blue plate specials at the Little Chateau! Before everything falls
through and Mother hides in the icebox and I stay inside so no one
can ask about the ceiling that opens to all the stars in the night sky.

30

A flashlight breaks my face in the toilet mirror,
my eyes lurking as I splash it cold and then take
a deep breath into the kitchen to Uncle's door
and knock until he looks down and yawns, "Huh?"
Then lift to my toes and scream, "Leave me alone. . . .
I'm not Izzy, I'm me!" Nobody blinks. Not even God.
Uncle doesn't crouch, scream or slam my head like
he did to Mr. Bein the bus driver who's always late,
he just steps back and shuts his door as if he never
once banged it, and his radio doesn't peep as I cross
the dark to pull the bottomless sea over my eyes.

PART III

I was sitting . . . with a young gypsy woman who did nothing, said nothing, only looked out motionlessly into the empty factory yard. . . . And on her face an impenetrable aloofness, a silence, a distance, which could not be reached by any word or any look from the outside world . . . I realized: That was what I always wanted to possess . . . for if I had it no one would be able to touch me. . . .

Gertrud Kolmar
(Letter of July 19, 1942, Auschwitz)

31

It's raining on our way to the beach so Father says, "Let's go to
No Rain Street where it's always sunny." He turns left and right
and stops on a dead end where he makes us sing: "Oh it aint
gonna rain no more no more oh it aint gonna rain no more the sun
will shine birds will sing oh it aint gonna rain no more no more."
Mother sighs as Grandma squeezes her eyes shut and says, "Now
he thinks he's God!" But sure enough sunlight spanks the pavement
2,000 watts! Hallelujah! Father did what God thought only he could!

32

The Dubinsky brothers dance the kazatsky atop a mountain
of old sinks and glittering glass, their arms folded like crucifixes,
chests heaving like cannons. Father says only the Russians think
dancing is kicking and spitting vodka while breaking dishes on
your head, only the Russians prefer tables to floors for dancing
and lovemaking. Only the Russians get stuck with their arms
crossed and right leg stuck out until Monday morning when
it's not showing off but showing up, bright and early, to get kicked
all the way back to Saturday night, which stands waving a red lamp
at the end of eternity like a Cossack singing, Dance dance dance
for all you're worth, which is nothing, not a goddamn thing!

33

My bar mitzvah is going to be in The Grand Ballroom
of the Sheraton Hotel. Mother says: We live behind a junkyard
and can't afford cement in our basement but he's throwing
the biggest party since Moses heard voices. This is *our* opportunity
to show everyone we're alive and kicking, Father yells, anyone
can rent a back room. But why pay ten years for one night,
she yells back. To have a night to remember, he says, she thinks
too small, debt is how you establish credit, the more the better,
that's why he keeps buying new machines, doesn't own insurance
or belong to a temple—he wants to owe everyone, even God.
All I want is a bowling party, for it all to be over with . . . at night
Mother eats tuna fish out of a can, with a spoon, sighing. . . .

34

I'm looking at picture books and stick Van Gogh down
my pants and walk out Sibley's department store when
a man grabs me and calls my parents. I pray for Mother
but Father comes, and doesn't say anything until we're
in front of our house. "Your bar mitzvah's in five months
and you don't even know Hebrew. I'm inviting bosses and
councilmen. Don't make a fool of me, understand?" I do,
but he doesn't. I wasn't stealing a book, but all that ecstasy.

35

One Saturday morning I find Mr. Schwartzman turning
on a piano string in his closet, his eyes drained of experience,
while I, and what's left of my childhood, get stuck in one place.
The world, he quoted Buber, permits itself to be experienced,
but has no concern in the matter. I'm as tall as he is, though
his feet don't touch the ground. Even now I don't understand
why he put his suit and tie on but not his shoes or socks.

36

When I start bawling, Mr. Leonard, my seventh-grade teacher,
keeps me after school. We were reading how every species
overproduces because only the strong adapt and I wondered
if Mr. Schwartzman was too weak. "Every memory leaves
a bruise, a terrible doubt," he said when I asked why he stared
at the ground when he walked. "Cioran, a crazy Carpathian,
said consciousness is a disease and Gertrud's mind attacked her
like a hyena. Thinking is what's unforgivable, be afraid of yourself...
I stare because I can't stop looking for scraps of food..."

37

Singing Al Jolson, Father shaves with a great splashing,
eyes blinking, fat bottom lip thrust out, hiking his pants
as he tells the mirror all the great things he'll do that day. . . .
Chasing or chased, he doesn't stand still long enough
to hear what he's thinking, Grandma says. Five foot one
and bald as the chickens she boils Fridays, nose pitted,
barrel chest worn high over his buckle, fear is the secret
to success, he says, naming all the big shots afraid of him.
He makes this look, cocks his eyes, "Be interested only in
what *you're* saying." He asks me how I feel about what he
thinks, then comes over and turns around to answer himself.
He stuck his thumb in a button machine, didn't even blink
as the blade sliced, then bought an old Ford with the insurance
and painted it yellow and called it The First Yellow Cab Co. of America
after The First Church of Christ in the middle of Main Street.

38

Three times a week Rabbi Runes comes to tutor me
and cough up phlegm in the sink Grandma scours
the minute he leaves. He stinks of tobacco, his teeth,
fingers, beard stained yellow. He screams if I look at
his hairy moles until Mother says I'm sensitive and
high-strung (my muscles tied too high and tight?) and
he nods, Shore shore, and sucks a Parliament to ash.
My birthday is in one month so he threatens to hang me
next to his photo of Rebbe Friedlander, head of the Big Shul,
who's as good as I'm evil. Every time Grandma opens a door
he breaks wind to show her what a piece of dreck she is.
When he leaves she screams, "God sends him to spit on
my dishes and still he's not happy, he has to leave a stink
that chokes even the dead. . . ."

39

The new girl at the end of the alley likes to smolder,
Billy says. She's from Czechoslovakia, where nobody
ever amounts to anything. We're in back of her Pa's pickup
on our way to Canandaigua. Czechoslovakians never smile
but take their clothes off as soon as they get to a lake.
"Yur advanced for yur age, I hope?" she says. It's October
so the trees look forlorn and stubborn like Grandma after
she bathes. I do what she tells me but Czechoslovakians
are never happy. "Know that Hildebrand kid?" she says
on the way back. "Ask him to come visit me. . . ." I don't
know why, but I do. Then I watch the Dubinsky brothers
unload bedsprings, yelling Russian. Like Czechoslovakians,
they're here twenty years and still can't speak English. One
comes over to pee in our yard and I yank the mesh fence back
and let it wave . . . until he's running backwards, screaming
something kulak. Next door, old man Haas looks up and smiles.

40

Billy Sanders lives above a funeral home and stinks
like dead people. He smokes Lucky Strikes and wears
a leather jacket to scare everyone. His Dad's face ends
below his nose even when he wears teeth, that's why
his Mom, Miss Finger Lakes 1948, left last year. His Dad's
a janitor at DuPonts where Father has vending machines
and now he's yelling because Father got him fired after
he told everyone we live around the corner. Father tells
everyone we live in the suburbs so I shouldn't be here
and now Father is banging on the door and Billy yells,
"Go out the back window!" so I do and climb down
the trellis and twist my ankle and limp across the alley,
my name following me around shadows, the big red moon
hanging an inch or two above my head like a yo-yo. . . .

41

"A Cossack attacked you!" Grandma screams. I'm scraped red
and my breath breaks my chest. "Who's after you?" Mother cries
as Father's car slams the curb and she pushes me and Grandma
into the toilet. "Where is he!" Father screams up the walk.
I yank at the window but it won't budge and my hand explodes
into the lightbulb so nobody has to see what's happening. "God—
what did I ever do to you?" Grandma says. "Get out of my way!"
Father yells. "Leave him alone or I'll call the police!" Mother cries.
"The police!" Grandma says. "Now he'll burn the house down!"
"He lied to me! A hundred times I tell him not to go there, does
he listen!" "Touch him and they'll put you in jail!" "What did you do,"
Grandma asks, "hold a mirror to his face?" Mother screams out
the front door so the neighbors should know he's trying to kill me
and Father kicks the icebox as Grandma nods at the ceiling and sighs,
"He who lies in a sty shouldn't be surprised when he's eaten by pigs."

42

I don't know anyone to invite to my bar mitzvah
who doesn't wear black leather so I invite everyone
in my Sunday dance class. Mother takes me to Sibley's
to buy shoes and cuff links and Father to the head tailor
at Fashion Park (cheaper by two) and Mother buys us
socks with coat of arms on the ankles. I learn to box-step,
bunny-hop and Mexican hat dance while Father invites
the entire Democratic Committee, even our Republican
barber who's a councilman, and borrows money from
all four younger brothers who must stay, he insists, at
the Sheraton because they're too proud to let him pay.
Mother talks to him when he's asleep because that's
when he listens, and Uncle has taken a bus ride across
the country so I can go to the attic anytime I want,
but mostly I sit watching the snow bury Cuba Place,
as if it doesn't want anyone to remember everything
that happened to us. . . .

43

I dream I get up in the dark to wake my sisters Hana,
Sarah and Rebecca, my brothers Zacharias, Israel,
and the infant, Simon. Nobody knows where we're going,
only that we must leave this place forever. We pack
what we can carry and pull in one cart and Mother
is trying not to cry. Have faith, says Father, we are larger
than what we know and we know only the past and soon
we will live in the future and celebrate my bar mitzvah
in a new home. Outside, the dark is breathing and I see
Moritz the tailor and Modecai the scribe and Rabbi Sachar
and his wife Hester who are trying to appear hopeful
as others come carrying torches, yelling and pushing,
and Mother stumbles and Father grabs her and Israel lifts
Rebecca who is holding Simon who is crying because
the dust is rising like a cloud of locusts and now everyone
is moving through the darkness beyond the city toward
the sea which is shining on our faces as others come out
of the shadows and there he is, Moses, high on a boulder,
waving for everyone to gather and Father lifts me high
on his shoulders to see all the gleaming faces and everyone
is singing—Dayeinu Day-einu—and Father squeezes me
and Mother is smiling and I am not afraid, we are so many,
and the night flees behind the hills as the sun rises out of
the sea like the face of God, and everyone is singing. . . .

44

My first morning as a man I practice with a razor,
like learning the piano, Mother says, it needs practice.
"Bubbe, did you brush your tooth this morning?" I ask,
everything's too quiet—krrraccckkkkkk goes her rocker—
"Even dogs won't piss on your grave!" she yells. Mother
comes in the kitchen wearing her new emerald gown
and best fake pearls, her hair stiff and shiny, eyes and
cheeks so polished and dusted I forget to be scared. . . .
"Well, bar mitzvah boy, how do I look, okay?" Great,
I say, putting on my suit and boiled-white shirt and blue
silk tie and black buckle shoes that snap like crickets.
Father comes out in pinstripes and a red polka-dot tie,
his big bottom lip thrust out. "Help him knot his tie," says
Mother, so he yanks at me, yells to stop moving, stands
back to look in the mirror, where, his hand on my shoulder,
he smiles at himself. . . .

45

We're all dressed but Grandma won't get in a car
on Shabbos so the neighbors can enjoy seeing what
lousy Jews we are. Father yells and Mother pleads
but Grandma hugs her ratty sheared beaver. "Ma, please,
you want us to be late for his bar mitzvah!" "For Chrissakes!"
Father screams, "the only ones who care if you drive
is us!" She stamps and Father pounds the hood as I go
over and say, "Bubbe, it's Sunday, we go to the beach
every Sunday." She shrugs as if she knew all the time
and climbs inside and we go down Rauber Street up
Hixon to Thomas and down Widman back around Hixon.
"Why don't we go straight there?" I ask. Mother sighs,
"Because he has to surround everything."

46

"We're not going to the beach, we're going to hell,"
Grandma says. It's not light yet when we get to the Big Shul
where two old men in long coats and black hats stamp
the front steps. The regulars, Father says, penguins.
One waves and Grandma screams, "They saw us driving!"
We go through the big doors carved with prophets
and cherubs into the marble lobby, Mother shushing
Father and Grandma squeezing my hand numb. I know
where I'm going but not why. Where is more important,
Mr. Schwartzman said, but everyone has an opinion about
why, even if it's only to ask why we're where we are.

47

Rabbi Friedlander shakes my hand. "You know your
Berakhahs and Haftorah?" I nod and he smiles. "He's
going to be a solid man, I can tell from the eyes,
don't worry, he'll make you proud," he tells Mother.
Then to Father, "You understand after he completes
his first Aliyah you go up to recite the blessing—Barukh
She'pturanee May onsho shel zeh, which means 'Blessed
is the One Who has freed me from the punishment due
this boy' . . . which means two things: with this blessing
the father is no longer responsible for his son's sins and
the father's failures no longer burden his son . . . understand?"
Father nods. "This calling up is a passage to adulthood,
your blessing his awakening, his liberation . . . from you!"
I shake as Rabbi Friedlander puts his arm around me.
"Be frightened. Today you begin to respect your fear."

48

Father's brothers, Uncles Hughie Teddy Al and Louie,
argue who is taller smarter makes more money, all
bald, short and shushed by the sextons from the bimah
as Rabbi Runes comes over to say what a genius I am
and Mother and Grandma smile down from the balcony
where God wants women to sit, Grandma says, because
if the ceiling falls only men survive. God doesn't understand
women, she thinks. She's one and understands nothing
about herself. Up there under the stained glass windows
and domed ceiling, Moses holds the Ten Commandments,
looking down from the glass clouds, where I want to be,
with all the women. . . .

49

"Since I was a boy in Krakow a bar mitzvah is my
favorite ceremony," Rabbi Friedlander says in front
of the Torah Scroll, as Mother smiles from the balcony,
along with Moses, King David and Saul.... "My father
David, sister Rebecca and brother William were all
still alive before the pogrom . . . now each year I awaken
to manhood to be tested again, as everything is a test
of God's love, even looking into the mirror, the boy
peeking through my old man's eyes, still frightened . . .
therefore"—now he looks at me—"I am happy to
welcome up to the Book to give his Aliyah blessing...."
Legless, I walk to the bimah where the sextons step
aside and the rabbi whispers, "Good luck, my boy,"
and, my eyes shut to not see all the faces, I listen
for the words to come out of my mouth, like breath....

50

He didn't hate himself, Mr. Schwartzman said,
he was just tired of the arguments in his head.
"Jews argue to change only their own mind
and everyone on Cuba Place is forgotten, left behind,
except you, my boy. You have time." He said this,
his musical hands on my shoulders, two days before
I find him hanging. These words, my bar mitzvah gift.

51

Mother smiles from the colored lights as
words scrape up my throat and come out
my mouth—I'm singing the blessing before
the reading of the law—"Borchu es adonoi
hamvoroch . . . Boruch adonoi hamvoroch l'olom . . .
Boruch atto adonoi, elohainu melech ho'olom,
asher bochar bonu mikol hoamim . . . adonoi . . ."
the rabbi singing too, then the congregation—
"This is the Torah which Moses placed before
the children of Israel . . . a tree of life to those
who take hold of it . . . its ways are pleasant and
all its paths are peace . . ." the words singing inside
and outside my body—"O Blessed art thou, Lord
our God, King of the universe . . . Creator of all
the worlds, who sayeth and performest, who
speakest and fulfillest, for all thy words are true
and just . . ."—tears in my mouth, hot and sweet—
"Have compassion . . . for it is the source of our life . . .
Blessed art thou, O Lord, who makest Zion rejoice
in her children . . ."—singing to Mother whose hair
is yellow fire—"Gladden us, Lord our God . . . bring joy
to our hearts . . . that his light should never go out . . ."

52

I find in Mr. Schwartzman's German Bible, in Ezekiel,
a poem, "Gog and Magog," he wrote in Yiddish:

Is it better to suffer in the house of mourning or in the house of feasting?
Free the flock of prayers stuck in my throat like sighs or run with the dogs
down the thirty thousand roads to hell? Bury myself in death as death
has buried me in life or remember and atone for nothing? To ask for comfort
at the graves of the unknown or kneel before the memory of the pious dead
who lay piled one upon another in a burning pit, each a blessing a sacrilege
a plea wafting like black smoke from the last fire in the bowels of heaven

Lord!

53

"Rest now and let your father say his blessing—you
sang like an angel, an angel," Rabbi Friedlander says
as Father moves up to the Book and takes a big breath
and cries out, "Blessed is the One Who has freed me
from the punishment due this boy . . ." and steps aside
as the rabbi moves forward and back and I lift off
the floor into the air and rise toward Mother, high
above the rabbi and Father, until I'm swaying in and
out of the glass light, turning above the bobbing heads
and exploding hands as the men sing . . . " . . . *mazel tov
und simmun tov, simmun tov und mazel tov* . . ." their feet
and hands jumping as Father and his brothers dance,
singing " . . . *simchah simchah* . . ." the words lifting
around me as I float out of my body into the glassy fire . . .
and beyond . . . into the eyes of God. . . .

54

A boy has one bar mitzvah but becomes a man
many times, Mr. Schwartzman said when I wondered
if I'd be any good at being one. It wasn't the biggest
bar mitzvah, but big enough. Father argued all night
with his brothers, even while waltzing Mother,
her eyes shut, as if afraid to see her happiness.
I danced Grandma around a cake shaped like the Empire
State Building and a chopped liver Eiffel Tower. "Smile
for posterity," the photographer said, as Father and I
clinked glasses in our Fashion Park suits, rooster-
crested shirts, white carnations in our lapels, "and look
thankful." . . . the way Father looked bursting into my room
each morning full of pep and high hopes, yelling, "Up and at
'em, we gotta get a jump on 'em, kiddo!" . . . yes, us against
the world . . . all of us, the living and the dead, wandering
in an endless epiphany in which only our grief belongs to us,
and what remains of our desire to colonize heaven.

PART IV

And all the rivers ran into my soul.

Gertrud Kolmar

55

Our story ended sooner than any of us expected.
The background had to be filled in, how we came
to be here, what we wanted, believed, originally.
According to the guidelines, the foreground provides
perspective while the background is where we bury
our illusions. Back there in the ancient mist, steaming
with innuendo. Why was our thinking so circular, tribal,
why weren't we more ironic, philosophical, sympathetic?
There's not enough evidence to explain our importance.
Perhaps the background goes on too long, there's too
little self-regard and we end abruptly, in the middle of
an unexamined story. Nothing we did mattered, finally.
No one understood what we intended to mean. We simply
stopped, the silence spilled over us like a sigh, the light
faded, discord ended, the curtains closed and we were left
sitting at the table, in darkness, our mouths agape. . . .

56

Why? This is everyone's favorite question. No one ever says:
Because our bags are always packed and we hear footsteps
on the stairs. Because the dark feels unwashed and incomplete
and Maimonides said, "When the Messiah comes war will end,
God's blessings will be on all men." Because we have a God
who never dies and never comes and it's three in the morning
and I'm walking a crying baby around, singing lullabies Grandma
sang to me. Because I expect nothing and what I expect defines me.
Because the world exists without us but without us it is nothing.
Because all my life I've been afraid of the next page. Because
nothing is explained and my old bedroom shadows are thriving
and the floor tilts west toward Lake Ontario where all the snow
comes from. Because it's getting late and I'm in bed, waiting
for Mother to come kiss me good night, like she promised.

57

I travel 100 miles on a bus to work in Manhattan where I tell people
what I think about this and that and then 100 miles back to my family
in a coma of shiny black lanes. This morning my brain watches a hearse
stuck in traffic on the eastbound side of the highway, the driver staring
into the tumult of a defunct December Tuesday. I've forgotten where
I'm going or why, though once I believed I knew. I'm afraid to think
beyond the phone lines and houses full of performing souls, each a single
beautiful spark stuck and fading in this strange infinite procession.

58

"I was always ready to do penance," Gertrud Kolmar wrote
before going to Auschwitz. How easily the tongue swallows its lies,
Mr. Schwartzman said. After he yanked himself from the dead,
he was an empty shirt, a barbed-wire fence, broken black wings
flying over a steaming landscape, a calendar of lost names,
an endless prayer for the dead . . . Gertrud sang, "Oh burn . . . your
inmost secret . . . let your progeny, the vulture-demons, circle endlessly
above the towers of death, the towers of silence. . . ." Once he believed
in civilization: Goethe Heine Kant Bach; celloed in Berlin's Philharmonic,
hummed Mozart. . . . Once music was "joy unceasing," a train journey
with a new season passing silently outside each prodigal window.

59

The man off in the far right corner of the painting isn't lost,
or even bewildered, he's determined to undo a great wrong
that happened down in the bottom left corner when he was
young and innocent of what was going on in the foreground.
He always wanted to go north but was too frightened of what
those in the south might think. Now he's stuck in a winter scene,
waiting for something to change. If anything, his appetite
for contrition has increased, so he remains in this tiny corner,
foreshortened and vague, a small piece of a larger picture.

60

Its eyes open, feet curled as if still holding something cherished,
the dead bird lies under my study window. "What kind is it?"
my son asks. "A winter bird of some kind," I say, knowing
it's my job to name things. "Why did it die, Daddy?"
Because it had faith in visibility, in the distance it had come,
the tiny fate involved, I think, but say, "It was tired, Eli."
We bury it under the stately cedars, marking it with stones
we found at the ocean. Then stand there, in the silence
no one understands, or wants to name.

61

The men and women who used to be my friends—where are they?
They've disappeared into the past which now feels lower,
less significant. Once everything felt so necessary, inevitable.
What happened to all our enthusiasm for ourselves? Suddenly
it's later than ever before and soon we'll all be gone, not one
of us left to remember what we couldn't forgive about ourselves.
Why we wanted to swallow God, knowing he would swallow us.

62

"Look out!—Mama's mad again!" our son yells out
the car window as my wife backs into the driveway,
wheels spitting, the buckled baby's eyes popping as
our dogs cower under a pointillism of euphonic leaves,
all of which appreciate the magnificence of her wide-
slung spondees as a whirligig of sleeves and pant legs
fly spread-eagled out our windows into the tremble of
the October sky, as I recite Elizabethan madrigals: *Oh
what a plague is love, how shall I bear it, she so molests
my mind, I greatly fear it.* . . . Yes, I, righteous bell tower
of complaint, who snores like Beowulf and keeps everyone
waiting as I feed the dogs 'something a little special,'
only I can make her this mad, and now, homeless and
fleeced, a hermit crab angling sideways toward Paradise,
bow, scrape and obey the unforgiving Torah of her ferocity!

63

Everyone's life is eventful. I hoist hundred-pound
sacks of coffee beans with a few caffeinated rats
and surprised snakes and then volunteer to protest
Port Chicago, where all the napalm gets shipped from,
New Year's Eve, 1967. Drive over the Golden Gate
across narrow ever-darkening roads, a VW bus packed
with rollicking ids, bumping over the countryside.
Stoned vigilantes freezing our shadows off round
a puny fire, we get punched, ridiculed and ignored
while the napalm keeps flowing east. Our honeymoon
with God is over. The world refuses to love us enough
so we quote Nietzsche: "Escape from the bad smell!
Escape the steam of these human sacrifices! Only
where the state ends, there begins the human being. . . ."
The sky opens its accordion pleats and it's the New Year,
but we haven't escaped anything, in fact, we barely
have time to say good-bye or wish ourselves luck.

64

The glass in our attic window wasn't real stained glass
but colored bottle glass, the kind you saw in all
the old houses on Cuba Place. Displaced glass used by
displaced people to affect an aura of good fortune
and civility. That's why we watered, hoed, and surveyed
our gardens with such devotion, pleading with God
to do right by every peony, cucumber and turnip, why
every Saturday men shined old Chevys and Plymouths
with beeswax and vinegar, and every spring women sang
in ten languages while hanging wash and picking cherries,
blackberries and peaches, and all of Rochester was one vast
walloping stink of lilac covering every walk, porch and fancy
with a pungent cloud of purple and white petals, why
American flags waved in every yard and men in overalls
and shirtsleeves whistled the national anthem, straining
to hear the Yankee game buried deep in static, why so much
was expected from a place where everyone was more than
themselves, where, no matter how far down you started from,
you began again from the beginning, with the same Godful longing. . . .

65

After Mother died we drove around Cuba Place,
up Rauber and down Hixon to Thomas, and around
Widman to the liquor store where the Big Shul used to be.
The cake shaped like the Empire State Building, that Father
insisted on, is the only thing about my bar mitzvah that
interests Eli. "Where's everyone in the stories you tell me
at bedtime?" he asks when we stop in front of my house.
"Living in the past," I say. Yes, even Billy Sanders, who wore
his hair in a DA and died in Vietnam. "No," says my wife,
"they're all dead," meaning: it's time to say good-bye.
The windows are boarded up, the Dubinsky brothers'
junkyard is an empty lot, and the big oak that stood
outside my bedroom window is a hole in the ground.

66

We need a new car, my wife reminds me. I sit at my desk,
open books, scratch my head. One needs to be practical,
take money from here, put it there. Everyone knows how
to do this. But I can't. I hate all those numbers marching
around like high-school bands. I hate being precise. Also,
I love my old car, it's so loyal, patient, manufactured.
It drove us to Maine on our honeymoon and through
a blizzard when my wife was in labor. It's not a living thing,
it has an engine, not a brain, a transmission, not a soul.
It doesn't remember singing the Stones' "Satisfaction"
the night Mother died, watching the ocean swallow
everything. It knows it's time to leave, that it's falling
apart, rusting. But I can't bear starting over again.
At night I go outside and reminisce, like an idiot.

67

Mother's Yahrzeit is on the 6th day of Av 5758.
Praise the living light and sing the name,
her secret private name, in no one's ear but mine.
Praise the evening of the day before the endless night.
Leave nothing behind, forget no article of clothes or candlestick.
Praise the night, which gives nothing back,
not even her name which will not pass this way again

Lord.

68

It was only possible to live in the past, where life is organized,
Martin Buber said. But all those stories swallowed by the earth,
all those dreams rotting in unmarked graves, all those souls
defeated by the rain . . . "Yes," Mr. Schwartzman sighed,
"they live in the past, like stowaways."

69

This morning I'm tired of the same newspapers, and arguments.
I'm tired of sticking the same legs into the same pants,
the same hands poking out of the same sleeves, going west
and then east, heating up the same tea, watching the same sun
rise over the same horizon, the same trees shedding the same leaves.
Tired of climbing the same stairs to look out the same window
at the same street, tired of shaking the same hands, opening and
closing the same doors, dreaming the same dreams, saying hello
good morning happy birthday I'm so sorry please forgive me.

70

At camp in the Connecticut woods my wife slow danced
to "The Long and Winding Road" in a polka-dot dress,
the cool lake air breeze on her cheeks as Richie's breath
gurgled in her ear, his sweaty hand snaking along her waist,
egging her north then south on the splintered deck. . . . I shift
the baby's weight, listening with our five-year-old son as
she explains how she bowed to fit her head to his shoulder,
her eyes closed, the same gray eyes that close for me, closing for
that twelve-year-old moron, her legs swaying as they do now,
the same blossoming in her cheeks, the glow of her raisin hair
as he kissed her, her first, there, under the canopy of floating stars,
the music and lake stars swooning, all of it now forever lost
deep in the scented woods of a Connecticut evening.

71

Late at night, in bed, my wife remembers Juan
who told his dying father he was dying too, and
had joined the Catholic Church so they could be
friends in heaven. She loved his stories about his
father's chocolate factory, how all Spain stunk of it,
the bullfighters he painted and loved not so secretly . . .
She says her name the way he did, softly, on the tip
of her tongue, as if tasting her soul . . . I understand,
ten years is a long time to love someone, and be
young together. After he died all his friends came
to see the film he made about the waiting room
of an AIDS clinic, "One Foot on a Banana Peel,
the Other in a Grave." She'd tell him everything
and he'd sit there, at his drafting board, listening
to her every word, as if it were precious.

72

The woman beside me on the jitney weeps into
a cell phone, "You're leaving me!" Every seat
is taken, it's late, and I'm tired so I rehearse
objections as she cries, "Billy! You love the way
I swim! You love my eyes!" I try an old distraction
trick: my dog Rusty runs off, it's my birthday and
beautiful Miss Crittenden, my fourth-grade teacher,
is leaving to get married. . . . "Hear that?" she cries,
ripping a magazine. "It's my heart!" Father dies bankrupt
and Mother returns to her old job as a filing clerk. . . .
"That time you saw the cuts on my wrist and asked
if I'd do *that* over you and I said no? I *was* lying."
I leave home and wander alone for thirty years. . . .
"I'm coming back to an empty house?" I stutter, lisp,
apologize too much . . . "Billy, please, a little mercy . . ."

Last Sunday my son got tired of skating so we walked
around the cemetery by the pond and stopped to read
a poem called "Free Mercy" inscribed on a stone in 1688,
about a boy who died at sea "innocent and happy," and
I wondered if it meant one shouldn't have to pay for it,
and we stood there, my wife, son, the baby, and me, each
a tiny piece of free luck, and all the kids skating behind us,
laughing, as if Miss Crittenden would never leave them.

73

"In the camp," Mr. Schwartzman said, "infinity was a comfort.
Now it's an assembly line, soup cans buttons shoes faces on TV . . .
like the lines of men women and children marching into the woods
to the ravine when the crematorium broke down, all their stories
of regret and triumph, their pleas to remain human a moment longer . . .
an infinity without heaven or hell, just endless blackness, beyond
which there's nothing, not even an idea to wonder or worry about. . . ."

74

My five-year-old son and I are watching TV
a few minutes before his bedtime. It's harmless
enough, a remake of *The King and I,* with elephants
and generous sunshine. Suddenly men are hanging
from trees, the light is gray and the music menacing.
I can't find the remote and feel around under the sofa,
bang my head, curse to immortalize the moment,
as dead men turn in the Siamese wind and our dogs,
thinking I want to horse around, head-butt me. Did I begin
my new life too late? I wonder. Now the happy elephants
are back, the world as it should be. But Eli isn't smiling.
"Daddy, why were those men hanging from trees with
arrows sticking in them?" Panting, I try to appear Kingly.
"Well, different cultures bury their dead differently."
Ah, what a vision before bedtime! I carry him up
the stairs toward what I pray are good dreams.
But I am dizzy, as if from turning in the jungle night,
my chest punctured and surging with the kind of
remorse only great happiness brings.

75

I dreamed my sons disappeared. We were watching
Peter Pan and I looked around like a blind man.
I awoke and peered into the darkness of my hands,
which have always belonged to someone more dour.
My sons were in the next room, asleep, but I had to
contend with the prospect of life with these hands,
and an entirely new order of things.

My bones aren't what they used to be; my eyes ache,
as if I've been reading an ancient text by candlelight.
My back and knees creak. I'm happy if the car starts
and I can walk the dogs along the ocean which looks
a little less robust. It replenishes itself with stretching
and long cleansing breaths. The sun is another story.
It's beginning to show its age. Perhaps we've enjoyed
enough springs and everything is getting a little redundant.

77

I'm on the jitney reading Tadeusz Borowski's
"This Way for the Gas, Ladies and Gentlemen,"
which I'm teaching tonight, God knows why,
when the jitney fills with smoke and pulls over
and we all push to get out and stand on the side
of the highway, watching the sky blacken. A woman
who has twisted her ankle and a man who stepped
on his glasses argue loudly with the attendants.
A moment ago, along with Borowski's character,
I cleaned bodies out of cattle cars, to eat, get shoes,
survive. It was a beautiful fall morning, leaves just
beginning to surrender their dignity. Now cars pass
like dust-shrouded souls as the black wings of
a great absence erase what remains of ours.

78

In the dream my milk curdles and I float
within the half parenthesis of the horizon.
I forget to set my watch back and my bills
are past due and I'm elected to the Chamber
of Commerce, my photo on the front page
of its newsletter, surrounded by the corrupt face
of truth. Nothing has been decided yet a terrible
mistake has become law. I stand for nothing;
I'm an anthology of small ideas. In the dream
the future is outlawed. Even God votes against it.

79

"All real living is meeting...," Martin Buber said, "true beings
are lived in the present, the life of objects is in the past."
It was Mr. Schwartzman's ambition to live in Buber's mind
like a grand hotel high in the Swiss Alps, not exactly heaven
or God, but far enough away from where we live our real lives.

80

The Old Stone Cemetery isn't right on Ridge Road,
where I remember, but a side street near Lake Ontario.
It'd be better to bury everyone together but this is
a Jewish cemetery so everyone's scattered. Mother
is next to Father but Grandma is three strangers apart
from her husband, who probably planned it this way.
No one can find Uncle's grave, Mother's revenge, a flat
stone planted somewhere north of her, in uncut grass.
A few Schultzes but a shtetl-full of Bernsteins, Kreigers . . .
it doesn't matter, no one ever called anyone by their name.

81

I wish the dead would take their bodies with them when they die.
I wish they would not leave them behind. I wish they would take
their dreams and streets and cafes. That they would understand why
we cannot say or do with anyone else what we said and did with them.
Why we cannot forgive them for leaving us behind.

PERMISSIONS ACKNOWLEDGMENTS

Some of these poems first appeared in the following magazines, to whom grateful acknowledgment is made: *Crazyhorse*; *Denver Quarterly*, *Forward*, the *Gettysburg Review*, *Harvard Review*, the *New Yorker*, *Pequod*, *Poetry Daily*, *Slate*, *Triquarterly*, and the *Yale Review*.

I also wish to thank Henry A. Smith, translator and editor of *Dark Soliloquy: The Selected Poems of Gertrud Kolmar* (New York: Seabury Press, 1975), from which I have drawn a number of lines.

Finally, thanks to Carl Dennis, Abby Wender, Grace Budd, Daniel Slager, my editor Drenka Willen, my agent Georges Borchardt, and especially my wife, Monica Banks, for their help and generosity